Cambridge English Readers
· ·
Starter Level

Series editor: Philip Prowse

The Girl at the Window

Antoinette Moses

D1250157

CAMBRIDGE
UNIVERSITY PRESS

CAMBRIDGE UNIVERSITY PRESS
Cambridge, New York, Melbourne, Madrid, Cape Town, Singapore, São Paulo

Cambridge University Press
The Edinburgh Building, Cambridge CB2 8RU, UK

www.cambridge.org
Information on this title: www.cambridge.org/9780521705851

© Cambridge University Press 2007

This publication is in copyright. Subject to statutory exception
and to the provisions of relevant collective licensing agreements,
no reproduction of any part may take place without the written
permission of Cambridge University Press.

First published 2007

Antoinette Moses has asserted her right to be identified as the Author of the Work in
accordance with the Copyright, Design and Patents Act 1988.

Printed in India by Thomson Press (India) Limited

Illustrations by Debbie Hinks

A catalogue record of this book is available from the British Library.

ISBN 978-0-521-70585-1 paperback
ISBN 978-0-521-70586-8 paperback plus audio CD pack

No character in this work is based on any person living or dead.
Any resemblance to an actual person or situation is purely accidental.

Contents

People in the story

Grace is a girl in 1815, and then a girl in a picture.

Sue is a young mother in 2001.

Sammy is Sue's baby girl.

Tommy is Grace's boyfriend.

Mary is Grace and Tommy's baby.

Places in the story

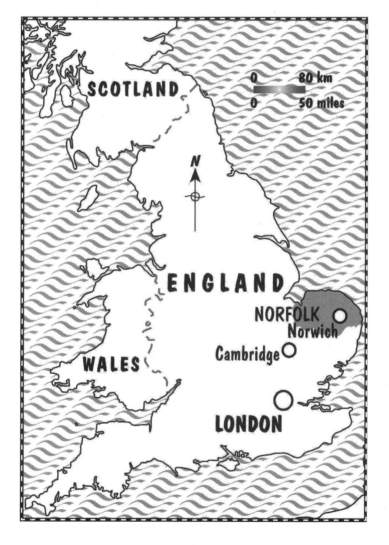

Chapter 1 *Don't take my baby!*

Grace: 1815

'Tommy! Goodbye. I love you!'

Tommy's going away. He's sixteen and he's a soldier. He's going to fight Napoleon.

I'm sad without him. But he's going to come home to me. And we're going to marry and live here. We're going to be very happy.

* * *

My name is Grace and I live in Norfolk. I'm sitting at the window and I'm waiting. Waiting for Tommy.

I know a song. It's a happy song and I like singing it. I'm singing it to my baby. My baby's inside me, but she can hear me. I know that. I know she's a girl. We're waiting for Tommy.

'Your father's going to come home, Mary.' I call her Mary. I look out of the window. In my head I see him. I see Tommy and he's looking at me. He has a red jacket and he looks very young. My Tommy. I sing, 'My Tommy's coming home to me.'

*   *   *

It's nine months now and the women are here. Mary is coming. The women are in front of my bed.

'Good girl, Grace,' they say. Then they say, 'And again. And again. That's it.'

And out you come, Mary. You're very, very small. And you're red and beautiful, and I love you. Oh, I love you!

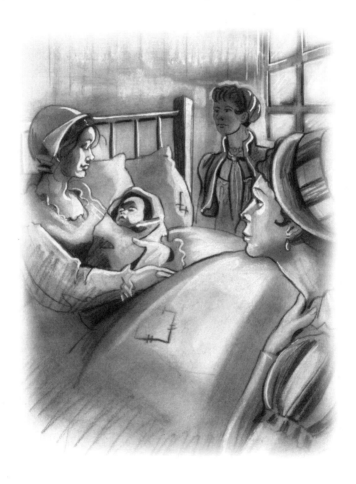

Then the women say, 'This is a beautiful baby. We're going to find a good home for her.'

'But Mary's my baby,' I say.

'You're a bad girl, Grace,' the women say. 'The baby doesn't have a father.'

'Tommy's the father,' I say. 'Tommy's going to marry me.'

'Tommy's dead,' they say, 'and you're not married. The baby comes with us.'

'NO! Where are you going? What are you doing? That's my baby. You can't take my baby away! Tommy's coming home. He's going to marry me. Mary! MARY! Where's my baby? I want my baby!'

* * *

This is my house. I'm waiting for my baby. People come and people go. People live here and people die here. But I'm always here. I'm waiting for my baby.

*   *   *

I can hear a baby now.

'Come to Grace, little one. Come to Grace. Grace is waiting for you.'

Chapter 2   *We love this house*

'Hello, Mum. It's Sue … What? … Yes. I've got a new home. It's a small house and it's only £250 a month … Yes, Mum, I'm here now and it's really beautiful. Sammy likes it, too. She's smiling. You're going to love it.

'What? ... Yes, Mum. The house is very old ... Yes, I know. But it's really cheap ... Why? Because it needs a lot of work ... Yes, of course there's a bathroom, but it's really cold and dark. I'm going to make it all white ... Yes, Mum. I am thinking about Sammy. She's going to be very happy here. She's going to have a nice room with a big window. There's a tree outside. Her bed can be near the window. She's watching the tree now. Can you hear her? She's laughing.

'Yes, Mum. I know you can't get here. I understand. It's OK. You have your work. But I'm going to be happy here. Sammy and I are going to be OK. We love this house.

'Why are you asking about Pete? I'm not living with Pete now … No, Pete doesn't know I'm here … Why? Because I don't want him here. You know why … No, he's not going to change. Pete is Pete. He's never going to change. He's never going to work. He just drinks … Yes, I know you don't like him. You always say that. You're right. You're always right. What can I say? Pete's not a good man. I know that now … No, I don't know. Why do people marry? … Love? No, I don't love him now, but he is Sammy's father. He's always going to be Sammy's father … Yes, I'm going to talk to him, but he's not going to come here … Because I'm happy without him.

'Mum, can you hear that? It's Sammy. She's laughing again. There's a picture in this room. It's a really nice picture. There's a girl at a window. She's really pretty … Yes, it's a really old picture. The girl's very sad. I think she's waiting for someone. Sammy loves looking at the picture …

'No, I know Sammy's a baby and babies can't understand pictures. But listen. She's laughing. She's happy here. I'm happy here. Everything's going to be OK. Bye, Mum.'

*   *   *

'Hello, Sammy, my darling. You're looking at the girl in the window. She's a pretty girl. Who is she?'

Chapter 3 *This is my house*

Grace

I'm the girl in the picture and this is my house. My name is Grace. I'm always here. Sometimes people come here. They come into this room and they say, 'It's a nice house, but it's very old. It needs work.'

I don't want them to come here.

Sometimes they see me. They say, 'Look at that picture. It looks old. There's a girl at the window.'

Then they say, 'Isn't she pretty?' or, 'She's very sad.'

I'm the girl at the window in the picture. Am I pretty? I don't know.

The picture is in a room and the room has a window, too. I look out of the window in the picture and I see the window in the room. And I look out of the window in the room and I see a tree. I see the tree in the wind. The wind blows the tree. *Whoooooooo*. I watch the wind and I listen to the wind. I love listening to the wind.

People come to the house and they come into my room. *Whooooooooo.* I blow and then the room's very cold. The people say, 'There's something I don't like about this house. It's cold. It's really cold.' Then they go away. And I'm happy.

Today a man comes to the house with a girl. The man finds people to live in the house. He comes here with lots of people. I blow *whoooooooo* and then the people don't come again. But this girl has a baby. The girl is pretty; she's seventeen or eighteen. Her baby's very small. I think, 'This is going to be my baby.' I don't blow *whoooooooo.*

The girl talks to her baby. She says, 'This is a beautiful house. Yes … yes it is, isn't it, Sammy?'

I say hello to the baby and the baby can hear me. She makes a happy noise.

'You're happy here, Sammy,' says the girl. 'You like this house.'

'It's very cheap,' says the man to the girl. 'You're going to be happy here.'

I sing to the baby and she laughs.

'Sammy likes this house,' says the girl. The baby laughs.

'Yes,' the girl tells the man. 'Yes, I want this house and this is going to be Sammy's room.'

YES.

Chapter 4   Something's happening!

Sue

'No, Mr Price, I want someone today … Yes, today. Today isn't tomorrow … Yes, I know you have a lot of work. I know I don't have much money … Yes, I know you're cheap and you're helping me. But you can't start something and then stop it. The wiring is bad – really bad. And I have a baby in this house … What? OK, Mr Price. Tomorrow. Tomorrow morning. Goodbye then.'

*   *   *

'Hello, Sammy darling. How are you? Mummy's very angry because the men aren't here today. No, Mr Price can't come today and his men aren't doing our wiring. And Mummy isn't happy. No, she isn't. Mummy is really angry.

'Sammy? Look at Mummy. Come on, Sammy. Don't look at the picture. Mummy's talking to you. Why are you looking at the picture? I think I'm going to take you into my room today. You come with Mummy.

'Ow! What's that? What's happening? There's no-one here, but … I don't understand. Ow! Who's there? What's happening?

'Help! I don't like this. Sammy! Come with Mummy. There's something bad in this room and I don't like it.'

*   *   *

'Hi, Mum, it's me, Sue … No, I'm OK. Yes, I know you're working. Well, there is something … I don't know what it is, but there's something. It's this house … What? I don't know. Just something … I don't know. It's not a happy house. And the wiring is really bad … Yes, Mr Price's men are going to come tomorrow … Of course I'm thinking about Sammy. I'm her mother. But what can I do? I don't have any money. I can't go to a hotel. Are you going to give me money for a hotel? No … Then I'm not going to a hotel … No, I'm not going to ask Pete for the money. I don't want him here. I don't want him to know I'm here. You know that.

'Sorry, Mum, Sammy's crying. Bye, Mum. I must give Sammy her lunch … No, it's not easy … You're right, it's not the house, it's me. Tomorrow I'm going to laugh about it. But today's a bad day. OK, Mum. Bye.'

Chapter 5 *Sammy is my baby*

Grace

This isn't good. The girl, Sue, is taking the baby into her room. But this is Sammy's room. Sammy's with me; she's my baby now. I don't like that name. Sammy's a boy's name. But she's a girl, a beautiful girl. Mary's a pretty name.

Ah! Sue's putting Sammy into her bed. She's here with me again.

'Hello, Sammy. You're my baby. Yes. You're smiling at me. I can see you.

'Oh Sammy, I'm very sad. I want my Mary. But now I have you and you're not Mary. Where's Mary? Where's Tommy? I'm waiting, waiting. And I'm very sad.

'Don't cry, Sammy. You're a very good baby. Yes. I'm going to sing to you. You like my songs. I'm going to sing and you're going to sleep. You're my baby now.'

*   *   *

What's happening? What's that noise?

It's a fire! The house is on fire.

'Sammy! You must come with me. Come here, out of your bed. I have you. Grace is going to take you.

'Don't cry, my little darling. I'm here; Grace is here. You're with me now. Everything's going to be all right. Grace is going to sing to you.'

Chapter 6 *Fire!*

Sue

'Is that 999? Fire, please. Quickly. Hello? Please, help me! My house is on fire! Please come quickly! My baby's in the next room and my bedroom door's on fire ... Yes, it's The White House, The Street, Eastham. It's on the left. It's a small, white house.'

Oh! What's that noise? The fire's really bad. I must get my baby. Sammy!

'Yes, I'm listening to you. But please help me! You must help my baby! I'm in my bedroom and it's on fire. The door's on fire and my baby's in the next room … Yes, I'm going to listen to you … Yes, I can stop shouting and listen. But I can't get to my baby. It's going to be too late …

'Yes, OK. I'm on the floor by the window now … Yes, I'm going to wait for the firemen. But please come quickly!'

* * *

'Yes, I'm listening. The firemen are here? Yes? But where's my baby? I can't …'

Chapter 7   *I can leave now*

Grace

'Sshh. It's all right, Sammy. I'm here. Grace is here and nothing bad is going to happen. You're beautiful, Sammy. My beautiful baby. The fire's very hot, but it's not going to come near you. I'm going to sing to you. You love my singing.'

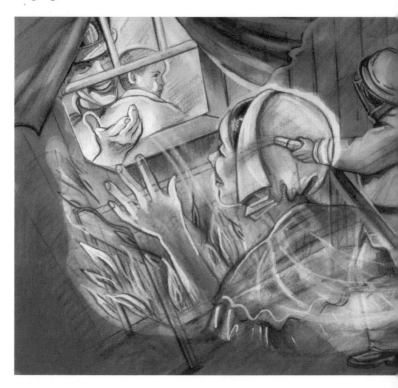

The fire's really hot. I can feel it. But I have to be here with Sammy.

'I love you, Sammy. You're my baby.'

I can hear someone. It's Tommy!

'Tommy, where are you? It's me, Grace. I'm here. I can see you now. I can see you and Mary. You're waiting for me. After all this time. I'm coming! I'm coming!'

But what about Sammy? I can't leave Sammy.

Now there are men here. They have water. They're putting water on the fire. It's all right. I can leave now. Everything's all right.

'Tommy, can you see me? It's Grace. I'm here. I'm here.'

Chapter 8 *We're waiting for you*

Sue

'Mum? It's Sue. I'm in the hospital. I'm OK.

'Where are you? ... On the train? One hour? Oh, good! I really want to see you. Oh, Mum ...

'Yes, Sammy's OK. Yes, I feel all right now, but I can't talk very well. Yes, I'm all right ... The house? No, there's no house now ... Yes, a very bad fire ... Yes, the wiring ... Sammy? She's OK ... No, I don't understand how. The firemen don't understand how. But the doctors say she's OK ...

'Mum, do you really? You want me near you? You're going to take me home with you? Oh yes! Yes. I need you, Mum ... I love you, too. Please come. We're waiting for you, Mum.'

AUG 2 6 2011

Cambridge English Readers

Look out for these other titles at Starter level:

The Penang File
by Richard MacAndrew
The English Prince is in Penang, Malaysia. But
so is Sergio, and Sergio wants to kill him. Can
Ian Munro find Sergio before it is too late?

ISBN 978-0-521-68331-9 paperback
ISBN 978-0-521-68332-6 paperback plus audio CD

What a Lottery!
by Colin Campbell
Rick loves music and wants to be a rock star.
But he has no money and his wife leaves him.
Then he wins the lottery. Is this the start of a
new life for Rick?

ISBN 978-0-521-68327-2 paperback
ISBN 978-0-521-68328-9 paperback plus audio CD

Let Me Out!
by Antoinette Moses
John makes a robot and calls him Nolan. Nolan can
do anything John wants. But Nolan isn't happy …

ISBN 978-0-521-68329-6 paperback
ISBN 978-0-521-68330-2 paperback plus audio CD

www.cambridge.org/elt/readers